Exercising My Fingers is as Easy as ABC

by Taylor Belich, MS, OTR/L

Illustrated by Toby Hanna

Dedication

This book is dedicated to my mentor, Sandra Cooley. The time I spent learning from you was not only profoundly impactful to my professional career, but also incredibly enjoyable. I will always cherish the time we spent working together. I wanted to express my heartfelt thanks for being such a wonderful mentor. Thank you for believing in me, challenging me, and sharing your extensive knowledge about Occupational Therapy in a school setting. The time and effort you invested in me has been invaluable. Thank you for being a constant source of inspiration and wisdom. The lessons I've learned from both our OT students and your mentorship laid the foundation for something truly meaningful, and for that, I'm forever grateful.

I need to exercise my fingers from my pinkie to my thumb
So I can write, color, and play for all the days to come!
It can be as easy as ABC
Read this book and you will see!

A is for Add with your fingers ...
2 + 3 = 5

B is for Build a tower with your hands and make it go up really high

C is for Clap your hands together like clap, clap, clap

D is for Duck puppet
that says
"quack, quack, quack"

E is for Exercise your fingers and move them all around

F is for Finger push ups off the ground

G is for Good luck sign where your fingers are crossed

H is for High five your friend sitting across

I is for Interlock your fingers, turn them over, and wiggle them like so

J is for Join your hands together to make a turtle that crawls slow

K is for Knock
knock knock on the
door

L is for Love in sign language to tell someone "I love you more!"

M is for Make a mask with your fingers to disguise your face

N is for Now fly with your hands like you are flying to space

O is for Okay sign
to let people know
that you are
all right

P is for Pinch like you are a crab squeezing tight

Q is for Quiet shhh...
like it's time for a nap

R is for Rock paper scissors to decide the match

S is for Snap until your fingers go numb

T is for Tap each
finger to your thumb

U is for Up your thumb goes in the air

V is for Volunteer
by raising your hand
while in your chair

W is for Wave
your fingers about

X is for X marks the spot no doubt

Y is for Yoga hands to get in your zen zone when you are stressed

Z is for Zero, because there are no more letters left!

Now my fingers are as strong as can be
It is as easy as ABC!

About the Author

Taylor Belich is the author of the highly acclaimed book "Calming My Body is as Easy as ABC" and a dedicated full-time Occupational Therapist. She is an Auburn University graduate with a Bachelor of Arts in Psychology and a minor in Human Development and Family Studies. She obtained a Master of Science degree in Occupational Therapy at Alabama State University. She primarily works in a school setting, serving elementary, middle, and high schools in the Lee County area in Alabama. She also works in other OT settings such as acute inpatient, outpatient, skilled nursing facility, private practice, as well as mental health short term and long term facilities when school is not in session. She has a passion for helping others improve their quality of life and increase their independence by encouraging them to reach their goals through creative interventions. She prides herself on providing client-centered, occupation-based interventions that she tailors to her OT clients based on their needs and abilities. She wanted to combine her experience as an Occupational Therapist with her love of writing to create books that are suitable for all children no matter what exceptionalities they may have.

Resources Page

Author Website:

To learn more, follow me on social media @taylormade.OT on Instagram, Facebook, and TikTok for Occupational Therapy tips and tricks!

www.ingramcontent.com/pod-product-compliance
Lightning Source LLC
Chambersburg PA
CBHW041559120626
46551CB00002B/257